Life Undecided

Shayne Nicholai

Published by Shayne Nicholai, 2024.

LIFE UNDECIDED

First edition. December 25, 2024.

Copyright © 2024 Shayne Nicholai.

ISBN: 979-8230401100

Written by Shayne Nicholai.

Table of Contents

Some of these pieces of writing contain content that may be triggering to certain individuals. Please be kind to yourself as you proceed. All the love in the universe.

-Shayne

5 Seconds

If the fighting inside me would ever stop
If I could only stop myself from going down
Then maybe life would be a little bit easier
And maybe love would be a little bit easier
The bruises and scars that I've given myself
Can never match the pain that dwells inside
And the only thing I can think of, the only thing I can think of
Is to live 5 seconds
And then 5 more
And pray, I'll pray that I can make it through
Oh yeah I'll pray, I'll pray I can make it through
If the internal struggle would ever fade
If I could only stop the voices in my head
Then maybe I wouldn't hate myself
And maybe I could even love myself
The bruises and scars that I've given myself
Can never match the pain that dwells inside
And the only thing I can think of, the only thing I can think of
Is to live 5 seconds
And then 5 more
And pray, I'll pray that I can make it through
Oh yeah I'll pray, I'll pray I can make it through
The blades and the fires are taunting me, calling out my name
Oh and I pray, I pray I can make it through
Telling me I cannot survive, cannot go on without them
Oh and I pray, I pray I can make it through

I slip and I fall but hold on so tight, knowing just what it would do to my friends
Oh and I pray, I pray I can make it through
Oh yeah I'll pray, I'll pray I can make it through
The bruises and scars that I've given myself
Can never match the pain that dwells inside
And the only thing I can think of, the only thing I can think of
Is to live 5 seconds
And then 5 more
And pray, I'll pray that I can make it through
Oh yeah I'll pray, I'll pray I can make it through
Live 5 seconds
And then 5 more

And I'll Never Let Go

When I wake up beside you it's like
A dream that's finally come true
And though I know that dreams can never last
I can only hope it's not over too fast
And on that morn when I find you're gone
Down a road less travelled I can't follow you on
But til that morning I'll hold you tight
Every night until my dying breath has passed
And I'll never let go
Cause with you I'm flying
With you I'm gliding
Through a world I've never seen before
With you I'm not hiding
Who I am or who I was
There's only here and now my feet don't touch the ground
And I'll never let go
When I close my eyes at night
I'm no longer afraid of the dark
Because I know you're there beside me
There's no more need, no more need for crying
And should rain ever fall from my eyes
I know you'll be right there to hold me tight
And you know that I'd do the same
Forever and a day
And I'll never let go
Cause with you I'm flying

With you I'm gliding
Through a world I've never seen before
With you I'm not hiding
Who I am or who I was
There's only here and now my feet don't touch the ground
Cause with you I'm flying
With you I'm gliding
Through a world I've never seen before
With you I'm not hiding
Who I am or who I was
There's only here and now my feet don't touch the ground
And I'll never let go
And I'll never let go

Anger That I Know

Darkness
It's a constant presence
A constant pressure
In the back of my mind
In the hole in my heart
I can feel the emotion
Feel the anger
Lurking like a beast inside
Prowling
Pacing
Waiting for the little break
So it can come through
And it comes
Full force
No mercy
I feel that if I opened my mouth
Everything inside would come
And pour out of me
But it does not have an end
There is no end to emotion
It is a bottomless pit
Of writhing, squirming hatred
And love
And sadness
And pain
There seems to be no peak

Always a new level to reach
More anger
More hatred
More frustration
Of why can't I stop this
Why won't it end
Like two hands are reaching out
Grasping me in their grip
And holding me tight
No escape for the wicked
That's what it says
The only way to quell the anger
Is to bring the pain
Only with the pain
Will the anger fade
And then the tears flow
Is there a way
A way to control this
A bottomless pit of rage
That can spark from the smallest spec
A mere water drop
And a single ripple
And then I know nothing more
Naught but rage and red
Anger and hate
The desire to break
The desire to scream
The desire to cry
The desire to throw everything in my path
Watch it all come crumbling down
Around my feet
Not satisfied until everything burns

Down into the bare ashes of life
Life gone by
That is no longer here
When will the screaming stop
When will the tears stop flowing
When will the fists stop flying
When will the anger fade away
I can never know
Until the pain
Until the cuts
And the bruises
And the blood runs red
This is the anger that I know

Baring My Soul

Tears roll down across my cheeks
And I can barely breathe
Can you help me to escape?
This pain that's haunting me
I don't know where I am
Or where I'm supposed to go
It seems I walk this empty road
Forever on my own
The stars at night they shine so bright
Lighting the path in front of me
Though I stumble and I fall
Every moment I believe
Every moment I believe
The pressure of your lips
As they pushed against mine
Oh the thought drives me insane
A better love I won't find
Would you bury me beneath?
The mountains and the seas
I will never learn to fly
Until you mend these wings
If the angels came to earth
If they walked among man
What would they do what would they say?
Would they set me free again?
Would they set me free again?

And I lie here
Baring my soul
All I can do is pray
I'll find my way home
And I lie here
With my heart on my sleeve
Watching everything drain out
Bleeding for all to see
And I lie here
Beaten and broken down
Clinging onto long lost love
Cause it's the only hope I've found
The only hope I've found
The only hope I've found

Bittersweet

To kiss your lips now
Is but a bittersweet memory
Will I ever escape somehow
This pain that's taking over me
How can I feel at all
When my heart lies on the floor
Broken and trodden down
I feel alone and my screams ignored
I'm running in place, the world frozen in time
While everyone around, keeps moving on now
If I were to disappear, who would remember
That lonely boy there, crying with his head bowed down
I'm on the edge, clinging with clenched fists
Wanting to let go, but dreading the pain
If I scream loud enough, will I scream my last breath
If I fall far enough, will I take my last step
To see your face again
Would rip my heart in two
Yet I say I'm fine
Since you left me behind
When he holds you close
I just want to die
Cause you took my heart back then
And then you said goodbye
I'm running in place, the world frozen in time
While everyone around, keeps moving on now

If I were to disappear, who would remember
That lonely boy there, crying with his head bowed down
I'm on the edge, clinging with clenched fists
Wanting to let go, but dreading the pain
If I scream loud enough, will I scream my last breath
If I fall far enough, will I take my last step
I'm running in place, the world frozen in time
While everyone around, keeps moving on now
If I were to disappear, who would remember
That lonely boy there, crying with his head bowed down
I'm on the edge, clinging with clenched fists
Wanting to let go, but dreading the pain
If I scream loud enough, will I scream my last breath
If I fall far enough, will I take my last step
So if I scream loud enough, will I scream my last breath
And if I fall far enough, will I take my last step

Can I Believe

Standing alone
Watching the world fall apart around me
Tears fall down
Like blood flows through all of my veins
With each step
There's a fall and words carved into flesh
Where did this go wrong
Where can we get fixed
So many words spoken
So many things left unsaid
And I don't know where to begin
Choking on words
Never knowing where to start or end
Freezing up
Do we part or continue down this road
Chaos is all
All that's left of my mind now that you're not here
Where did this go wrong
Where can we get fixed
So many words spoken
So many things left unsaid
And I don't know where to begin
Wearing my heart on my sleeve
Could you pick up all the pieces
I'm not fine
I'm not okay

What makes love
When all I can think of is you
Can I believe in me
Can I believe in you
Can I believe at all now

Choking Me

Sleeping away the bitterness
Cause it seems like there's nothing left good to look forward to
When I wake up in the morning
It's always the same damn things that keep going down
Sleeping away the emptiness
Cause even though she's right here beside me always
It still feels like I'm alone
And I can't stand being alone
And I try
I try to look for the positive
But it seems
That sometimes that's just too much to ask from me
The sun may be rising
But I know it's gonna set eventually
So why
Can't I
Find something out there that's just for me?
Sleeping away the bitterness
Cause it seems like there's nothing left good to look forward to
When I wake up in the morning
It's always the same damn things that keep going down
Sleeping away the emptiness
Cause even though she's right here beside me always
It still feels like I'm alone
And I can't stand being alone
Sometimes

I have days that just make me afraid
To step outside
Because there's so much out there so much bigger than me
And I admit
Sometimes I blow things way out of proportion yet
To me
It feels
Like nothing is ever in proportion anyway
Sleeping away the bitterness
Cause it seems like there's nothing left good to look forward to
When I wake up in the morning
It's always the same damn things that keep going down
Sleeping away the emptiness
Cause even though she's right here beside me always
It still feels like I'm alone
And I can't stand being alone
And as I fight away the bleary eyes
And try to write in words
How I feel
Everything seems to choke itself
Everything seems to choke on the way
Everything seems to be choking me
Everything seems to choke itself
Everything seems to choke on the way
Everything seems to be choking me
Sleeping away the bitterness
Cause it seems like there's nothing left good to look forward to
When I wake up in the morning
It's always the same damn things that keep going down
Sleeping away the emptiness
Cause even though she's right here beside me always
It still feels like I'm alone

And I can't stand being alone
I can't stand being alone
(it's choking me)

Dance in the Dark

The dawn is breaking
It's the start of a brand new day
But my mind is stuck on yesterday
Stuck on yesterday, yesterday
Dwelling in darkness
I'm alone and I'm afraid
I can hear the voices calling
But I can't put a face to the sound
So if you're near me
Please reach out and hold me
Cause I'm falling, I'm falling down
I'm still falling, still falling from yesterday
So drop a step and move a little closer
We'll dance with the darkness 'til it's gone
Hold me close and whisper in my ear
I'm not alone, I'm not alone, not alone after all
So take a sip and break it down
All the walls that are keeping us apart
Let the light in, let the light shine in
So we don't have to dance in the dark

Haunting Melodies

haunting melodies
floating through my head
so many different tunes
all meshed together as one.
hands flow up and down a piano
so smoothly across the white and black
releasing the soul that belongs
to the owner of those hands.
different songs, different beats
so many tempos in my mind
yet eerily all are of the same type
sad and slow, soft and mellow.
fingers plucking a sweet melody
out of the strings of a guitar
letting the emotions ring loud and clear
and fill the room with their vibrancy.
words that come from the mouth
revealing it's heart to all who can hear
to all who can read what is said
the speaker is naked before them
unclothed and their heart
ripped brutally open to show
show all the pain that they feel
using the only way they know
how to let it all out
the only way they know to escape

through these words they are freed
and yet now for it they are judged
judged for what they feel
judged for what they see
judged for what they say
judged for how they think
judged for who they are!
...judged for who they can't be...
I can see the notes floating in my head
so colourful, so mournful, and so beautiful
I want to reach out and touch one so I do
it sends out ripples and releases a sound like a bell
that rings hauntingly in my mind
hanging there forever reminding me
the effect of an action is now forever present
they never truly go away, they are merely forgotten.
that is why people keep making the same mistakes
people before them do something and the effects are felt all over the
world
and everyone and everything is reeling in pain
praying that this will never happen again...
but the first moment that someone forgets the past
and does what the other did it starts again
the waves ripple and swell to exponential sizes
once again reminding people of what this world can do.
each ripple that occurs is like a note in my head,
a beat but never a rest to be found
never finding peace in this vacant hole
the one that fills me inside
that fills me till I have no room left for anything else
filled with vacancy.
I once cried out to the heavens for someone

for anyone to help me be freed
but nobody answered.
maybe they weren't home
but the point is...nobody was there
they said they'd be there
why weren't they there!?
they just left me there to drown in this flood
this flood of emotions that I cannot explain in words
I can only explain with tears and screams
letting myself bleed to provide more openings for it to escape.
this haunting melody is still there
ever present in my mind, never leaving me in peace
I open my eyes and it's there
I close my eyes and it's there
I open my mouth and it flows out
I close my mouth and it builds up inside.
maybe the hands on the piano could teach me
teach me how to be free
to let my heart and soul out
to give them a chance to recuperate
give them a break from always hurting
give them a chance to heal after being broken so many times
after being broken for so long.
the final chord of the song, so haunting
like a Halloween haunted house
that chord could be all the music that was played
and the whole place would be filled with mysteriousness
filled with passion and confusion and longing and fear.
fear of the inevitable
fear that one day the music will stop
and leave me in a place of pure silence
that will take away all that I hold close to me

just leave me alone with my fear
with my longing
with my loneliness
with my pain
with my sorrows
and with my regrets
with nothing to drown out the silence
nothing but tears
the tears that are shed because I cannot hear
nothing can overcome the overwhelming silence.
silence...
it's a thing that I fear so much
because silence means emptiness
and emptiness means loneliness
and loneliness means loveless
and to not be loved...
is a crime in itself upon the world
no one can exist without it
no one can understand it.
there are no words to describe love
just like there are no words to describe emotions
we can try but we will always fail
there are some things that words just cannot say
and perhaps some things are left unsaid
the silence can hear them
but the world cannot
the world is too busy listening to itself
so full of itself and not paying attention
what is the reason, then,
if we were able to describe love
if we were able to describe emotions,
what is the reason to, if there is no one listening.

no one but the silence that I fear
the melody that lingers
resonating it's haunting notes through my head
though at times it overwhelms me
it is better to hear it than to be deaf
wrapped in a cocoon of silence
unable to see
unable to touch
unable to feel...
unable to feel what we so long to be able to describe
love
and emotions
filled to overflowing with a void
a void that cannot be filled, and leaves no room within you
no room to feel
no room to reach out and start a ripple, in hopes of escaping this pain.

Fallen

The shining stars they call out to me
wondering just where I'm going now
another path with another chance
to make things right again this time
and I'm fallen, I'm fallen on my knees and I am
begging. I'm begging you to please not go tonight
cause I'm feeling all alone
I'm feeling naked and exposed
I'm feeling regret
I can't be with myself right now
cause I'm not feeling innocent
not feeling quite alright
I'm feeling despair
I can't be with myself right now
I can't be with myself right now
a dusty road that's all that's ahead
stretching for miles 'til you can't see
a barren wasteland crying for rain
crying just like me for another try
and I'm fallen, I'm fallen on my knees and I am
begging. I'm begging you to please not go tonight
cause I'm feeling all alone
I'm feeling naked and exposed
I'm feeling regret
I can't be with myself right now
cause I'm not feeling innocent

not feeling quite alright
I'm feeling despair
I can't be with myself right now
I can't be with myself right now
and then the rain falls down, and the earth rejoices
as the water rushed over this once dead ground
is this my answer? is this my clue?
should I be begging for forgiveness from you?
no parting waters, no burning bushes
just a light rain falling on my face
as I begin to run towards you
you're so far away but I will catch you someday
and I'm fallen, I'm fallen on my knees and I am
begging. I'm begging you to please not go tonight
cause I'm feeling all alone
I'm feeling naked and exposed
I'm feeling regret
I can't be with myself right now
cause I'm not feeling innocent
not feeling quite alright
I'm feeling despair
I can't be with myself right now
I can't be with myself right now

Just Break Me Apart

sometimes I feel lonely and unwanted in this place sometimes I feel I'll
never find the one the one person just for me and when I feel this I feel
it deep down inside I feel the emptiness I feel the darkness I feel it
clawing away inside clawing away in me like an artist carves the stone
shaping who I'll become and I feel so at loss of what I should do with no
one to hold my hand when I'm all alone in the dark and the dark is
consuming me the darkness devours all and it hurts in my heart it feels
like it's cracking up waiting to break into a million pieces and crumble
all over the floor as I lie here dreaming of someone to hold me and
someone to love me someone who will keep me safe who can help me
through this pain that's breaking me slowly it's breaking me so slowly
that I want it to just hurry up get it over with now and just break me
apart just break me apart

Just Leave It

The river flows
And twists and curves around the city
Where the lonely lights
Glisten on the rippling water
And the echoes
Of the empty hearts pass me by
And I
And I
And I feel that I should tell you
The truth about me
But at the same time
I'm scared to be let down and turned away
Should I tell you?
Give an ultimatum;
To take me as I am or just leave it?
The rushing wind
Blows invisibly between the streets
Making itself
Known to all who dare to step outside
And the screams
Of the broken voices reach my ears
And I
And I
And I feel that I should tell you
The truth about me
But at the same time

I'm scared to be let down and turned away
Should I tell you?
Give an ultimatum;
To take me as I am or just leave it?
But what if you say
That you don't want me
What do I do
With my broken heart?
And what if you say
That I am no longer yours?
What do I do
With my broken mind?
And what if you say
That you're fine with it
What do I do
With my broken life?
What do I do....? What do I do?
And I feel that I should tell you
The truth about me
But at the same time
I'm scared to be let down and turned away
Should I tell you?
Give an ultimatum;
To take me as I am or just leave it?
And I feel that I should tell you
The truth about me
But at the same time
I'm scared to be let down and turned away
Should I tell you?
Give an ultimatum;
To take me as I am or just leave it?
Just leave it

Just leave it
Either take me as I am or just leave it

Just Want Your Love

When I was young, I walked this road blindly
There was a God, never questioned, doubted anything
As time went by, the road kept getting colder
I cried for help, but I only got the cold shoulder
They preached the hope, they preached the loving
But when it came to being different, oh it was sinning
They would yell and they would swear, "it's not how God had planned."
Wouldn't even bother to talk, or try to understand
But if I could fly, fly into the midnight sky
What would you say? Would you be proud of me then?
If I'd continued to hide who it is that I am inside
What would you say? Would you be proud of me then?
I don't want to lie, because when I do I just want to die
Oh it tears me up, that I just want your love
I thought I would try just a little to open your eyes
Oh but it tears me up, cause I just want your love
I can deal with the stares; I can deal with the whispers
It's the unabated hate that makes me just want to pull the trigger
If God's so merciful, why are you so quick to judge me?
While you stand there in your pulpit saying Jesus wants us to be more
loving
There's one thing I could never really understand that well
How you could sit there while they condemned your own child to hell
Why won't you listen to me when I try to state my point of view?
When you raised me to always try to walk a mile in someone else's shoes
But if I could fly, fly into the midnight sky

What would you say? Would you be proud of me then?
If I'd continued to hide who it is that I am inside
What would you say? Would you be proud of me then?
I don't want to lie, because when I do I just want to die
Oh it tears me up, that I just want your love
I thought I would try just a little to open your eyes
Oh but it tears me up, cause I just want your love
But if I could fly, fly into the midnight sky
What would you say? Would you be proud of me then?
If I'd continued to hide who it is that I am inside
What would you say? Would you be proud of me then?
I don't want to lie, because when I do I just want to die
Oh it tears me up, that I just want your love
I thought I would try just a little to open your eyes
Oh but it tears me up, cause I just want your love
Oh but it tears me up, cause I just want your love

How Do You Talk to a God

How do you talk to a god you haven't been able to trust since you were a teenager?
How do you talk to a god you're angry at for leaving you alone when you needed him most?
How do you talk to a god who let you suffer for years from nightmares that you would kill your own friends and family and be left alone? That you would laugh while doing it?
How do you talk to a god you've spent the past 10 years running away from?
How do you talk to a god you're scared has abandoned and condemned you to know nothing but the darkness in your heart?
Who let you live so long in fear that the thing you fear the most is yourself?
So much so that you always end up pushing away everyone because you're scared you'll hurt them...
So much so that you begin to hate yourself...
When you want someone to love you, hold you, and kiss you...but are scared that if they ever found out who you are that they'll leave and you'll be alone again.
How do you talk a god who you feel has betrayed you?

I am Broken

What is faith?
If no one answers your prayers
What is hope?
When nobody is there
What is life?
If no one shows they care
What is the point in anything?
When you're all alone
And when you cry yourself to sleep at night
And hold onto your pillow tight
Wondering how it would feel to not wake tomorrow
What is the world made of?
And when you lie and say that you're alright
When you just want to give up this fight
Wondering how it would feel to end this life you've borrowed
What is the world made of?
What is love?
In an empty room
What is heart?
Too scared to leave the womb
What is pain?
Scars cover over every wound
What is the point in anything?
When you're all alone
And when you cry yourself to sleep at night
And hold onto your pillow tight

Wondering how it would feel to not wake tomorrow
What is the world made of?
And when you lie and say that you're alright
When you just want to give up this fight
Wondering how it would feel to end this life you've borrowed
What is the world made of?
How can I stop this bleeding inside me
How can I be who I was meant to be
If at every step
I am broken
How can I fill this emptiness
How can I feel any more than less
If at every step
I am broken
I am broken
And when you cry yourself to sleep at night
And hold onto your pillow tight
Wondering how it would feel to not wake tomorrow
What is the world made of?
And when you lie and say that you're alright
When you just want to give up this fight
Wondering how it would feel to end this life you've borrowed
What is the world made of?
And with every step
I am broken

I Dream

The night has come
The sun has fallen
I'm alone at the edge of the world
Watching the stars
Fade in and out
Crying for the angels as they fall to the ground
I dream of magic
I dream of peace
I dream of you watching over me
I dream of faith
I dream of hope
I dream of you never letting go
Close my eyes
Go back inside
To a time when I knew who I was
When every kiss
Landing on my lips
Filled me with dignity and filled me with pride
I dream of magic
I dream of peace
I dream of you watching over me
I dream of faith
I dream of hope
I dream of you never letting go
These emotional scars
You left on my heart

Will only soften and fade with time
When I'm with her
All of my hurt
Seems to heal a little faster, heal a little faster now
I dream of magic
I dream of peace
I dream of you watching over me
I dream of faith
I dream of hope
I dream of you never letting go
I dream of magic
I dream of peace
I dream of you watching over me
I dream of faith
I dream of hope
I dream of you never letting go
Never letting go
Never let me go

I Know

To stand at the edge of the world
And look back without regrets
The kind of life I wanted before setting out
On a brand new road of tests
But if you can't have one thing
And you can't have the next
Then what are you supposed to hold onto
When you have nothing left?
And when the heavens open up
And the rain starts to fall
I know I can smile once more
Knowing you'll be there
Standing right by me
And when the sun goes beyond the horizon
And the moon rises up
I know I can sleep soundly tonight
Knowing you'll be there
Holding me tight
To reach out to the brink
And stare into the endless space
While wrapped in warm thoughts of home
Forget the faults of human race
If they only look at the bad
And never look at the grace
Then how can they stand to stay standing there
Looking at the reflection of their face

And when the heavens open up
And the rain starts to fall
I know I can smile once more
Knowing you'll be there
Standing right by me
And when the sun goes beyond the horizon
And the moon rises up
I know I can sleep soundly tonight
Knowing you'll be there
And when the heavens open up
And the rain starts to fall
I know I can smile once more
Knowing you'll be there
Standing right by me
And when the sun goes beyond the horizon
And the moon rises up
I know I can sleep soundly tonight
Knowing you'll be there
Holding me tight

I'm Not Sorry

For once in my life the changes have aligned
giving me the strength to move on
And she never looked back to say I'm sorry
and never turned around to say goodbye
I think of all the times she lied
and I don't feel sorry...no I don't feel sorry
Because she ripped a hole in my heart right from the start
and she's looking at me like I can't see
the broken promises that she's made
and the scars that now won't fade
and I'm not sorry...
I let her go, put her in as a memory
a past time I might regret
I know I won't forget the nights we spent
thinking we were meant to be
but now i see that
she never looked back to say I'm sorry
and never turned around to say goodbye
I think of all the times she lied
and I don't feel sorry...no I don't feel sorry
I never tried to hurt you (so I'm not sorry)

Only So Many Times

Game over you lost it
You blew your last chance
I should have known that you're no good with romance
No more begging
No more "but, baby please"
I gave enough chances
as it is
Let me put into words how I feel
How everything about you doesn't seem real
I
Hate
You
And your stupid lies too
There's only so many times you can break someone's heart
And what you did to me, well I
I don't know where to start
Go ahead and say it
I'm not afraid
I'm never gonna see you again anyway
No more begging
No more "but, baby please"
I gave enough chances
As it is
Let me put into words how I feel
How everything about you doesn't seem real
I

Hate
You
And your stupid lies too
There's only so many times you can break someone's heart
And what you did to me, well I
I don't know where to start
You lead me on to believe that you cared
But did you really care?
Was I just being used
So that she'd get jealous and want you back?
How would you feel if i died?
If I shot myself tonight?
Would you care at all?
Baby let me know how it feels
To lose something so dear
Oh wait you already did....
Baby let me know what it's like
To have your heart shoved on a spike
Oh wait you already did.......
I think I'd swear to be alone
if it weren't for the fact
That I just can't handle being alone
And I can't do that
So listen up now
From here to forever on
I swear that I will never
Never ever date someone like you again
Let me put into words how i feel
How everything about you doesn't seem real
I
Hate
You

And your stupid lies too
There's only so many times you can break someone's heart
And what you did to me, well I
I don't know where to start

In my Hands is Only

there's a pop
and you're in
as everything inside begins to pour out
what's this?
this feeling?
i wonder what it's like to sleep forever
as life
pours out
sometimes you gotta wonder if it's now or never
to try
and hold on
but then you realize that it's far too late now
regrets weigh heavy on my mind
and everything that's left on the inside
I reach out just to see the light
and see in my hand is only a knife
I wonder who I wanted to be
there's nothing left that I can see
everything around me is closing in
all the lights are growing dim
like a flash
and it's gone
a feeling is a moment is a memory and
it's all
for one thing
do you cherish it forever or throw it all away

it's just
out of reach
so you scream and you shout and you burn it all down
down
to the ground
if you can't have it then nobody else can either
regrets weigh heavy on my mind
and everything that's left on the inside
I reach out just to see the light
and see in my hand is only a knife
I wonder who I wanted to be
there's nothing left that I can see
everything around me is closing in
all the lights are growing dim
and if this water turns to wine
what will it taste like?
and if these feelings inside of me
turn out not to be?
I guess it doesn't matter now
for as long as I wake up even with this knife in my hands
you'll be happy then
there's a pop
and you're in
as everything inside begins to pour out
what's this?
this feeling?
I wonder what it's like to sleep forever...

Insanity

this insanity makes me feel like I could lap up the blood of millions
while laughing with tears of joy in my eyes.
this dive into darkness makes the pain excite me and delve further
inside, away from the lie called normality.
I separate myself from god in order to be able to feel the horror that
lives inside behind the curtains of my mind.
the pain of separation is my punishment that I deserve for crimes come
and gone and yet to arrive.
the monster paces constantly and though I name thee anger it never
fades, ready to devour my soul and lead me to its' world.
the world I long for, the world I crave for....sometimes....
I want to bite into flesh and rip it off the bone, just to satisfy the needs
and quench the thirst.
to see faces writhing in pain amuses me and I could watch it all day
long.
caress the skin with the tongue and then bite down, let the blood trickle
down the throat, down the face, down the body.
and laugh as the scream
because they don't understand
that the insanity has got a hold on me
and inside I'm crying
wanting it to stop
for someone to kill me
to save me
to end me

Like a Piano

Shots fired and my heart
Is bleeding on the floor
Draining into the ocean
And dreaming of something more
Is there a god up there?
Surrounded by the stars
Or is it all just nothing?
Is it empty like my heart?
And I hear the universe
Playing us like a piano
Up and down the black and white
With nothing in between
And I hear the universe
Calling out your name
Longing for words once spoken
Longing again to be seen
Where has the color gone?
There's nothing left around
A flash of red on an apple
And a glimpsing of a sound
Meet with an elder now
For the memories of the past
Full of painful truths and
You're hoping it won't last
And I hear the universe
Playing us like a piano

Up and down the black and white
With nothing in between
And I hear the universe
Calling out your name
Longing for words once spoken
Longing again to be seen
And the stars cry out
I'm cold and I'm alone
Is there someone out there?
Whom I can hold
I reach out my hand
And withdraw quickly
For fear of being burned
This love is bittersweet
And I hear the universe
Playing us like a piano
Up and down the black and white
With nothing in between
And I hear the universe
Calling out your name
Longing for words once spoken
Longing again to be seen

Memories

The sun can't always last forever
sooner or later it has to fall
casting us into a world of darkness
stuck in a state of mindless wandering
I want to live in a world of pure black
not that there's such a thing as a black that's pure
but when you're surrounded by nothing but darkness
you're filled with such a calming feeling
So when the world comes crashing down
you won't feel a thing, you can die peacefully
And the world becomes just like the wind
you can feel it, but you can't see it
Because what you can't see can't hurt you
it's as harmless as a breeze, blowing through the trees
I'm locked in a room filled with shadows
a place where the lights will never burn out
The lights hit my eyes and I can feel them burning
I'm begging for someone to end my pain
Call me a fake or call me a liar
I believe some people are better off dead
'Cause in my sleep I see the world burning
everything's ashes in the end
So when the world comes crashing down
you won't feel a thing, you can die peacefully
And the world becomes just like the wind
you can feel it, but you can't see it

Because what you can't see can't hurt you
it's as harmless as a breeze, blowing through the trees
I'm drowning in these nightmares that flood my dreams
They all haunt me in my sleep
This dark rain falls and I'm trying to hold on
I'm writing you these words so that what I've seen doesn't come to you
in your sleep
'Cause everything that I never had
is everything that you deserve
Rainbows and birds that sing you lullabies
Let me lie still in my dark world
so that you can have the world of light
From afar I'll protect you every day and night
Please don't cry, don't shed your tears
it's not your fault that I'm not here
When you're sad, just think of me
and maybe I can make you happy
I'll always be here in your dreams
and all dreams are, are memories
am I a happy memory?
So when the world comes crashing down
you won't feel a thing, you can die peacefully
And the world becomes just like the wind
you can feel it, but you can't see it
Because what you can't see can't hurt you
it's as harmless as a breeze, blowing through the trees

Morning's Dawn

The world paints clear pictures in our heads
Fills it with lies, until we can't get out of bed
And then those very same people try to tear us down
Saying, "why can't you just be happy?" with big smiles all around
They can never understand the emotions that I'm feeling
I'm hanging off a cliff, and my fingers are slipping
Who will be there?
Who will grab my hand and pull me up?
Who will be there?
When I feel like I have had enough?
When I look at these scars, I feel nothing but shame
Because the world told me that it meant that I am insane
I tried to walk along the greener pastures
But I found myself thinking that nothing really matters
So I dug my own grave, and prepared for the fall
Who would even miss me? I'm no one at all
As I steeled my nerves, and I braced for the pain
I heard a voice cry out, calling my name
Are you there?
Will you grab my hand and pull me up?
Are you there?
'Cause I feel like I have had enough
When I look at these scars, I feel nothing but shame
But you're telling me that I'm not insane
You tell me that each scar is a battle that I've won
That I've gone through hell and back, and came out someone

The pain behind my eyes, you say, is proof that I've survived
But never forget the ones who didn't get a second try
So hold your head up, child, the darkness will fade
The night will always end and turn into day
While you may feel right now like you'll never see the sun
It's always the darkest before the morning's dawn
I will be there
To grab your hand and pull you up
I will be there
When you feel like you have had enough
When you look at your scars, you feel nothing but shame
But I am telling you, there is strength behind your pain
So though you may feel right now that you'll never see the sun
But it's always the darkest before the morning's dawn.

Never Regret

You can't have a melody without a harmony
You can't have faith without having doubt
You can't have regret without forgiveness
And you can't have any hate without having love
So hold tight to the ones who love you
And walk them through their darkest times
Never give up, never let them fall
And never regret what you cannot know
Memories are precious, so hold them dear
Enjoy every waking moment, every second that you share
And every night you sleep you'll see in your dreams
That the ones you thought gone are still in your heart
The shadows can be dark, and the road can be painful
But when you're not alone it makes it more bearable
To wander this path stumbling to find your footing
To know if you reach out, there's a hand right beside you
So hold tight to the ones who love you
And walk them through their darkest times
Never give up, never let them fall
And never regret what you cannot know
Let the ocean's mist spray on your face for an extra second
And inhale a little bit deeper next time
Revel in the fact that your heart is still beating
And that people surround you with love and care
Let this music take you to your world of fantasies
Let the rhythm match the flowing thrum of your blood

And each moment take a little step further
The dark will fade soon enough in time
So hold tight to the ones who love you
And walk them through their darkest times
Never give up, never let them fall
And never regret what you cannot know
So hold tight to the ones who love you
And walk them through their darkest times
Never give up, never let them fall
And never regret what you cannot know
Never regret living, for a moment at all

Nothing Left of Me

I'm here at the edge of my pier
Don't know where to go, feel so all alone
And I, I want to be free, from this misery
That's holding me down, put my feet back on the ground
And what do I do
When all that's left of you, is a hole inside me
And how do I see
When all that's left of me, is an empty shell
And I~ don't know what to say to you now
And I~ don't know how to breathe without you
And I~ wanna know what it's like to see you again
And I~ wanna know what to be without you
Cause there's nothing left
There's nothing left of me without you
Where did I go wrong
I treated you the best I could have
And tell me how, I could have done better
What I could have done right to make it last a little longer
How do I forget
The taste of your kisses that linger on my lips
Why do I remember
The touch of your skin as you held me tight
And I~ don't know what to say to you now
And I~ don't know how to breathe without you
And I~ wanna know what it's like to see you again
And I~ wanna know what to be without you

Cause there's nothing left
There's nothing left of me without you
And when I close my eyes
All I see is you
How do I forget, How do I forget
And when I close my eyes
All I hear is you
How do I forget, How do I forget
And when I close my eyes
All I feel is you
How do I forget, How do I forget
How does one forget something that was so good
How does one forget something they never want to
And I~ don't know what to say to you now

Not in Control

Somebody stop me
because I can't seem to stop myself
these scars are the proof that
I'm not the one that's in control here
and everything I am
and everything I was
has changed
nothing seems to go right
nothing seems to go my way
somebody please stop me
as I write these words I'm shaking
crying seems like a really good idea
I never like to worry all my friends
but I just can't seem to find a way
from going under
Somebody stop me
because I can't seem to stop myself
these scars are the proof that
I'm not the one that's in control here
and everything I am
and everything I was
has changed
nothing seems to go right
nothing seems to go my way
somebody please stop me
even though I have somebody who loves me

I can't seem to help feeling down from time to time
and it's in those moments that I falter
it's in those moments that the darkness creeps in
and starts taking over
Somebody stop me
because I can't seem to stop myself
these scars are the proof that
I'm not the one that's in control here
and everything I am
and everything I was
has changed
nothing seems to go right
nothing seems to go my way
somebody please stop me
(somebody please stop me)
somebody please stop me

One Day

Broken-hearted, that's the best time to write a song
You take all your feelings, and play 'em out with each strum
It ain't easy; sometimes I lie awake at night crying my eyes out
But I got friends who will pull me through
'Cause one day I'll be fine
Over time the pain will fade
It'll get easier to look at your face
And one day I'll get married
I'll find someone to love me
The way that I loved you...
'Cause my friends will pull me through
I stare in the mirror looking at my reflection
Wonder what it was that made me not good enough
I know it's stupid; but I just can't help wondering what we'd have been
But I got friends who will pull me through
'Cause one day I'll be fine
Over time the pain will fade
It'll get easier to look at your face
And one day I'll get married
I'll find someone to love me
The way that I loved you...
'Cause my friends will pull me through
I still want you, every inch of my heart aches
Thinking of you, and I don't even know why
I can't get you off my mind, and I can't even get a moment's rest
But I got friends who will pull me through

'Cause one day I'll be fine
Over time the pain will fade
It'll get easier to look at your face
And one day I'll get married
I'll find someone to love me
The way that I loved you...
'Cause one day I'll be fine
Over time the pain will fade
It'll get easier to look at your face
And one day I'll get married
I'll find someone to love me
The way that I loved you...
'Cause my friends will pull me through
'Cause one day I'll be fine
Over time the pain will fade
It'll get easier to look at your face
And one day I'll get married
I'll find someone to love me
The way that I loved you...
'Cause my friends will pull me through

Pocket Watch

There's a pocket watch lying on the desk
The second hand has long since stopped moving
Every second lost is a second wasted
Don't waste your life not having faced it
She lies on the floor frozen in time
Because time has forever stopped for her
But if you look so closely you can see her smile
Smiling 'til the end just like I remember
Every sunset and every sunrise
I'll see your smile, in the sky
Every morning and every night
I'll whisper to you, goodnight, goodnight
This rose has gone and wilted away
Just like the life of my dearest friend
But with every death there is new life
Rising up from the ground just waiting for its chance to shine
Every moment that I breathe I remember
That smiling laugh and taunting as she ran away
This time though she has run too far
To a place I know I can never catch up to her
Every sunset and every sunrise
I'll see your smile, in the sky
Every morning and every night
I'll whisper to you
Every sunset and every sunrise
I'll see your smile, in the sky

Every morning and every night
I'll whisper to you, goodnight, goodnight
And as the sun shines down from the heavens above
I'll know she is there watching over me
So I will remember, I will not regret
I'll live my life in a way she never could imagine
Because imagination is what you perceive
And I perceive you watching over me
With a smile and a laugh I could never forget
With that smile and that laugh I could never forget
Every sunset and every sunrise
I'll see your smile, in the sky
Every morning and every night
I'll whisper to you
Every sunset and every sunrise
I'll see your smile, in the sky
Every morning and every night
I'll whisper to you, goodnight, goodnight
Goodnight, goodbye

Pure

Trapped
Caged like a lion and pacing back and forth
I've lost my freedom and my means of escape
And so the pain just sits there, waiting
No way to get out, no way to release it
Because everyone's watching, waiting to see
Waiting to see if I'll do it, if I'll mess up again
And it leaves me with no place to escape to
Everyone fighting for my attention
When all I want is to hide away
Away from the eyes that are always on me
Staring
Watching me like a hawk watches its prey
And if I go more than one minute without paying attention
SNAP!
I get attacked
I can't go anywhere to hide, the eyes follow me
I can't do anything to escape
Not even sleep enables me to evade the eyes
They watch over me all night
As if - if they looked away, I would suddenly be gone
And it makes me think
Maybe it would be better
To let everything out at once, and be done with it
Rather than be forced to keep it in
Everyone says it's not good to keep it bottled in

But then they don't give me a way to let it out
They don't let me get it out
Hypocrites
If they want me to live, they should let me live
Not enclosed like some kind of zoo animal
That people can come and see when they want
With a big sign that says "suicidal tendencies"
And leave me to be stared at by doctors and observed by nurses
Like I'm some kind of guinea pig
In a zoo
Like I'm some kind of rare species
That's never been researched before
And they're not quite sure what to make of it
So they stare at me all day and all night
And in my enclosure I have no places to hide
Nowhere to slink beneath submissively
Is this how my life is going to be forever?
Will I always be trapped?
Or will I someday be set free...free to release what's inside
Because it's eating me up
And it really doesn't matter
Someday I'll be gone, no matter what they do
And it's up to them when that time will be
Sooner
Later
It doesn't make a difference to me
Because if I go, I won't feel anymore
And I won't have to care

Something to Believe

Struggling day by day to make it through
Taking small steps because I don't know what to do
Searching for a faith to cling tightly to
A belief I can call my own
A belief I can call my own
And I wish I could believe like I did when I was a child
To believe in a Lord and God and never doubt, never doubt
Unwavering faith is something we take for granted when we're young
And when you grow up and you're alone you just wanna cry out-
"Oh my God, are you up there?
Can you hear this simpleton's heart crying?
I want to believe in something to believe
I want to know if there's a greater good for me
Is there a purpose to my life, or am I just born to die?
If you can hear me, if you can hear me
If you can hear me, answer me please."
When you're so small it's like the world's trying to take you down
You cry out for a helping hand, but no one is around
And you wonder if you've even made a single sound
And you just feel so alone
You feel so alone
And I wish I could believe like I did when I was a child
To believe in a Lord and God and never doubt, never doubt
Unwavering faith is something we take for granted when we're young
And when you grow up and you're alone you just wanna cry out-
"Oh my God, are you up there?

Can you hear this simpleton's heart crying?
I want to believe in something to believe
I want to know if there's a greater good for me
Is there a purpose to my life, or am I just born to die?
If you can hear me, if you can hear me
If you can hear me, answer me please."
What happens to the hearts who stopped believing in hope long ago?
When the highlight of their day is watching their favorite TV show
Where has that childhood innocence gone, no one knows
What happens when you lose your soul?
What happens when you lose your soul?
And I wish I could believe like I did when I was a child
To believe in a Lord and God and never doubt, never doubt
Unwavering faith is something we take for granted when we're young
And when you grow up and you're alone you just wanna cry out-
"Oh my God, are you up there?
Can you hear this simpleton's heart crying?
I want to believe in something to believe
I want to know if there's a greater good for me
Is there a purpose to my life, or am I just born to die?
If you can hear me, if you can hear me
If you can hear me, answer me please."
And I'm just a boy trying to find his way in the this world
And I'm just a boy trying to find his place in this world
I'm just a boy, I'm just a boy, I'm just a boy, I'm just a boy, I'm just a
boy...and nothing more
I'm just a boy, I'm just a boy, I'm just a boy, I'm just a boy, I'm just a
boy...and no one more
And I wish I could believe like I did when I was a child
To believe in a Lord and God and never doubt, never doubt
Unwavering faith is something we take for granted when we're young
And when you grow up and you're alone you just wanna cry out-

"Oh my God, are you up there?
Can you hear this simpleton's heart crying?
I want to believe in something to believe
I want to know if there's a greater good for me
Is there a purpose to my life, or am I just born to die?
If you can hear me, if you can hear me
If you can hear me, answer me please."
If you can hear me, if you can hear me
If you can hear me, answer me please.

Sometimes

Sometimes, when I look into your eyes
I can see the pain that you're trying to hide
And sometimes, I can see into your heart
And I can see the scars from where it broke apart
And sometimes, when I see your smile
I can see the fear that you'll never be worth-while
I know the road can be hard to walk alone
And I know that life ain't easy
I know that sometimes you feel you aren't loveable
And I know the fear that breeds
When the darkness is filling up your heart
And you don't know what to do
Hold on, I'll be there for you
When your thoughts are racing, can't sleep at night
And you feel like you can't breathe
Hold on, I'll be there soon you'll see
I'll be there soon you'll see
Sometimes, when I lie awake at night
I fear the shadows cast by the moonlight
And sometimes, when I'm feeling lonely
I can't stop the thoughts saying, "If only..."
And sometimes, I worry that I'll never find love
And I worry that no one's watching from up above
You know the road can be hard to walk alone
And you know that life ain't easy
You know that sometimes I feel that I'm not loveable

And you know the fear that breeds
When the darkness is filling up my heart
And I don't know what to do
I hold on, and I wait for you
When my thoughts are racing, can't sleep at night
And I feel like I can't breathe
I hold on, 'cause you'll be here soon for me
You'll be here soon for me
When the darkness is filling up your heart
And you don't know what to do
Hold on, I'll be there for you
When my thoughts are racing, can't sleep at night
And I feel like I can't breathe
I hold on, 'cause you'll be here soon for me
You'll be here soon for me

Stifling Winds

I'm all alone
Just living in these memories
With no one to care
Waiting for a chance to breathe
This wind is so stifling
And I can't seem to gain any ground
So many paths so many choices
And bridges I can't get around
Waiting for a chance waiting for a moment
To try and take a step
And pray that I won't fall pray that I won't fall
Fall through the ground
Step by step day by day
Just trying to live
Trying to find something of worth
Something to give
This wind is so stifling
And I can't seem to gain any ground
So many paths so many choices
And bridges I can't get around
Waiting for a chance waiting for a moment
To try and take a step
And pray that I won't fall pray that I won't fall
Fall through the ground
This wind is so stifling
And I can't seem to gain any ground

So many paths so many choices
And bridges I can't get around
Waiting for a chance waiting for a moment
To try and take a step
And pray that I won't fall pray that I won't fall
Fall through the ground

Still Breathing

Can you hear me here?
Cause I don't think I can hear you where you are now
Are you the whisper in the wind?
Are you the rolling thunder?
As I stand here alone
I like to think
I can feel you
But the truth is I'm not sure
I can feel anymore at all now
Won't you give me a sign
Touch my face
So I know, that I'm still breathing
It's a glistening sunrise
And it touches my body oh so softly
Just like you used to do
Maybe the dark would give me some solace tonight
As I stand here alone
I like to think
I can feel you
But the truth is I'm not sure
I can feel anymore at all now
Won't you give me a sign
Touch my face
So I know, that I'm still breathing
Why can't you still be here?
You should be holding me close

Telling me it's all just a dream and it's almost over
Tell me why aren't you here?
Don't you care?
Tell god that I need you here with me
And as I'm falling apart....
I hear....you whisper
Calling my name.
And I know...that you're with me
Saying goodnight
Well my love I'll see you shortly
(wait for me.....don't let me wake up from this dream)
And as I stand here alone
I like to think
I can feel you
But the truth is I'm not sure
I can feel anymore at all now
Won't you give me a sign
Touch my face
So I know, that I'm still breathing

Suicide Letters

2am Sunday morning, she's still awake
Writing a letter to her mom and dad
This is what it says
"Dear mom, dear dad I love you,
That will never change.
But I'm writing this to you so you know
That you're not to blame"
"I'm sorry to do this to you but it's getting too hard for me to stay
You wouldn't believe what I hear in school, every single day
She placed her suicide letter on the bedside table
Next to the flickering candle lights
Shadows dancing on the wall, one of them starts to fall
Starts to fall
She lost all reason to carry on and she can't find any hope
Any hope at all
Took her fate into her own hands and now she's in a different land
A different land
That's why she wrote her suicide
That's why she wrote her suicide
That's why she wrote her suicide letter
6pm Friday evening, nobody's home
He's crying into his pillow and
He's all alone
"Why do they always do this to me?
I never did anything to them
But they keep doing it

Over and over again, dear mom and dad
I'm sorry to do this to you but it's getting too hard for me to stay
You wouldn't believe what I hear in school, every single day
He placed his suicide letter on the bedside table
Next to the flickering candle lights
Shadows dancing on the wall, one of them starts to fall
Starts to fall
He lost all reason to carry on and he can't find any hope
Any hope at all
Took his fate into his own hands and now he's in a different land
A different land
That's why he wrote his suicide
That's why he wrote his suicide
That's why he wrote his suicide letter
They placed their suicide letters on their bedside tables
Next to the flickering candle lights
Shadows dancing on the wall, one of them starts to fall
Starts to fall
They lost all reason to carry on and they can't find any hope
Any hope at all
Took their fates into their own hands and now they're in a different
land
A different land
That's why they wrote their suicide
That's why they wrote their suicide
That's why their wrote their suicide letters
That's why they wrote their suicide
That's why they wrote their suicide
That's why they wrote their suicide letters

Their Love

It's 4 o'clock in the morning
The telephone rings
It's the day you've been dreading
For the pain it will bring
No more hearing that laughter
Only the sound of your tears
No more happy ever after
You're drowning in your fears
But, my friend, don't you know
That even though you feel alone
Even though they may have gone
Their love will always be holding on
Nothing will ever fill
That empty space in your heart
But I know something that will
Keep you from breaking apart
So lean on me as you need
'Cause where you are I have been
I know the way and I'll lead
Until you can breathe again
'Cause my friend, don't you know
That even though you feel alone
Even though they may have gone
Their love will always be holding on
And my friend, don't you know
That you are never alone

I am right there beside you
And I know what you're going through
So, my friend, don't you know
That even though you feel alone
Even though they may have gone
Their love will always be holding on

The Next Step

Just like the raindrops
Falling down my window
You never stop until
You hit the floor
And broken now
You're struggling
To get back up
But the world's too much
And with the weight of the world
Your knees are shaking just standing alone
You can't imagine walking now
With each breath it gets harder to breathe
And with the weight of the world
You never know which moment's the last
And with bated breath
You take the next step
Never knowing the meaning
To take it slow now
All of the scars and bruises
Are visible for all to see
You don't show fear
Don't show regret
The past is the past
No more, no less
And with the weight of the world
Your knees are shaking just standing alone

You can't imagine walking now
With each breath it gets harder to breathe
And with the weight of the world
You never know which moment's the last
And with bated breath
You take the next step
Even if you don't know where the next step will take you
Even if you are scared to walk it alone
Even if sometimes it seems like it's too much to take
Even then, even then, you take the next step
And if I could just be like you
Like I've always wanted to
I could take the next step...and be with you

This is Me

Lying on the grass in the middle of the night
It's cold and dark outside
And it always seems to match the feelings I have inside
My heart is tuned to the emptiness
This circle of black that seems to surround me...constantly
Sometimes you see it
And sometimes you don't
But always it's there eating away inside of me
There are days
When I'm not sure that I can make it
And you get mad at me for saying these things
But this is me
Lying in bed next to you
Lost inside my head
Trying to find that passion that I used to have
In the end it always seems
That everything precious to me.....always leaves
Sometimes you see it
And sometimes you don't
But always it's there eating away inside of me
There are days
When I'm not sure that I can make it
And you get mad at me for saying these things
But this is me
And I can't help it
There are days I feel that magic is flowing from my fingertips

And there are days I feel that my soul is absorbing everything happy
inside
And there are days that waking up is the hardest thing to do...
But still I have to...because I know
That there's no guarantee that tomorrow will be the same
Everyday's a gamble
You never know what side you're gonna wake up on
Sometimes you'll wake up and roll over and go back to sleep
But other days you'll jump right up ready to take on anything in the
world
And you do.....because you know
That there's no guarantee that tomorrow will be the same
Sometimes you see it
And sometimes you don't
But always it's there eating away inside of me
There are days
When I'm not sure that I can make it
And you get mad at me for saying these things
But this is me
This is me
But this is....me

Time is Not Reality

Have you ever seen the sun rise on yesterday?
Tomorrow never comes, and today never came
Did the light shine on the path behind you?
So that you can't see where you're going?
But don't look back, cause you won't like what you see
It will crush all your hopes
And destroy all your dreams
Yesterday was but a moment ago
Life flashing before your eyes
Tomorrow has never existed
As time passes by
You're stuck living in the past
Look what you've done
Look what you've done
Have you ever seen a fire that doesn't burn?
Impossible you thought, but it's everywhere you turn
Did it roll across the ground creating life?
Blocking your way home?
But don't look back, cause you won't like what you see
It will crush all your hopes
And destroy all your dreams
Yesterday was but a moment ago
Life flashing before your eyes
Tomorrow has never existed
As time passes by
You're stuck living in the past

Look what you've done
Look what you've done

To Be Loved

hold me tight
just let me know you're here
whenever you're around
I feel like there's nothing to fear
hold me tight
please, don't let me go
I don't know what I'd do
if you left me here all on my own
I want to feel love
because I don't know what it's like
I feel so empty
is this what it's like to be dying?
your presence is magical
you always make me feel so whole
with you everything is right
and I know everything's under control
I want to be loved
I want to be held so tight
I want to be kissed
I want to be told it's alright
I want to know what it's like...to be loved

What She Truly Longed For

I fell in love with a girl
But I only knew her name
I tried to enter her world
But she just pushed me away
And the tears she cried at night
Continued to go unheard
She was drowning in her pain
Isn't it absurd
That through all the tears and all the sadness
Through all the anger and the rage
The only thing that she truly longed for
Was someone to hold her
There was something about the way she walked
That just drove me insane
There was something about the way she talked
I wanted her to stay
Her sad sorry smile
Broke so many hearts
But mine's been broken before
All that's left is parts
So she can't break me
If I'm already broken
Maybe we could fix each other
Or maybe I was just hoping
I thought if she gave me a chance
I could show her she's not alone

Love is anything but instant
Slowly you keep moving on
And the tears she cried at night
Continued to go unheard
She was drowning in her pain
Isn't it absurd
That through all the tears and all the sadness
Through all the anger and the rage
The only thing that she truly longed for
Was someone to hold her
Sometimes in the dead of the night
I can still hear her breathe
And so I close my eyes tight
Begging not to see
Because when she noticed me at last
It didn't matter that I was poor
And she decided at that moment
That I was worth dying for
Then I wake from a dream
And realize that it was me
I was the one who died
And she is still alive
Searching for her queen
She had no need for a king

Adventure

Let us escape from reality
Into a world of imagination
Where all of the trees
Are these bright, brilliant greens
And hues of sapphire alight the skies
Let us go on adventures
Into far off, distant lands
We'll fight off the dragons
And defend the flag and
Become a hero found only in lore
Let us traverse the stars
Stepping among the galaxies
A star's just been born
And in that moment, I swore
I saw hope come crashing out loud
Let us gaze into the future
And all the possibilities that arise
When every little path
Brings a fast-growing panic that
You feel only magic can solve
Let us look for the answer
In tarot, crystal, and time
In the peace that you've found
Others tell you you're bound
To hell for valuing all lives
Let us see through the mirror

And beyond the calling clouds
The haze is so tempting
Brings blissful forgetting
The darkness that's always around
So let us escape from reality
To the seas, I'm nobody now
The stormy winds blow
No one seems to know
When they'll die down again
Let us go on more adventures
Climb up to the mountaintops
Cold, frostbit, and iced
Wouldn't it be nice
To have a place to escape all my own
Let us fly through the stars
We'll leave no stone unturned
Exploration, discovery
Go back in time to find the
Exact time that the universe began
Let us look to the future
Try to find out just who we are
the self-doubt and the hate
don't have a role in our fate
In a world that we call our own
Let us seek out an answer
With fighter, cleric, or bard
A song or a spell
All our fears will dispel
We get stronger with every encounter
Let us go through the mirror
Self-reflection, the final boss
Ruminate is the aid

That hinders your raid
What's unknown is if you come out on top

Paranoia

Just a little boy
Whom they called a little girl
Running round trying to find out
Who he was in this world
Even as a child
Not a finger could be placed
On what he was feeling
So he felt nothing but disgrace
Paranoia and anxiety
Filled his every day
Now he knows nothing else
He knows no other way
From the laughs and the stares
At 6, 10, and 13
All the way through high school
His heart was full of hurting
Never knowing why
Someone would be so rude
He just didn't understand
How the world could be so crude
So, even though he was told,
"it'll be ok, it's fine"
He was always on the lookout
For when that becomes a lie
Because how could that be truthful
When they shower praise on those who do well

While he's stuck down inside
His own living personal hell
Who is he, who was he
Who should he be
"If no one feels the same, then,
Am I the one who's strange?"
He took in all that fear
And found someone who tried
But instead of building him
They destroyed him from inside
Just one hit, just one word,
Just one painful line
After all the fear
The accusations and the lies
"You will never be good enough"
"You will never measure up"
He took all those feelings
And buried them in a cup
It was the same damn words
He had told himself every day
Every minute, every hour
Since he was just a babe
"I will never be good enough,
Why can't I get it right?"
As he sits there and compares
Himself to everyone in sight
Everybody's watching and
Everybody's listening
Everybody's judging and
Everybody's whispering